First Person

A Poetic Narrative of Heartbreaks and Hallelujahs

Red Summer
Foreword By C.C. Carter

A Two Fingers Press Publication

First Person

Two Fingers Press- Poetry Division- November 2006

A Two Fingers Press Publication
1507 E. 53rd St Suite 112
Chicago, IL 60615

Copyright © 2006 by Red Summer

All rights reserved. Printed and bound in the United States of America. All rights reserved. No part of this book may be reproduced or transmitted in any form or by any means, electronic or mechanical, including photocopying, recording, or by an information storage system – except by a reviewer who may quote passages in a review to be printed in a magazine, newspaper, or on the Web – without permission in writing from the publisher. For information, please contact Two Fingers Press, 1507 E. 53rd Street #112, Chicago, IL. 60615.

Visit our Web site at www.twofingerspress.com for information on more resources for writers

The author and publisher verify that all slights of people, places, or organizations are unintentional. Any similarities to persons living or dead are unintentional and unrelated.

First printing 2006

ISBN 0-9777609-0-1

ATTENTION CORPORATIONS, UNIVERSITIES, COLLEGES, AND PROFESSIONAL ORGANIZATIONS: Quantity discounts are available on bulk purchases of this book for educational, gift purposes, or as premiums for increasing magazine subscriptions or renewal. Special books or book excerpts can also be created to fit specific needs. For information, please contact Two Fingers Press, 1507 E. 53rd Street #112, Chicago, IL 60615; email info@twofingerspress.com

Cover photo and design by Christopher Adams at Impakt Studio Chicago

Foreword

Look out world!!! There's a new femme in town, wearing stilettos, a push up bra and sporting army fatigues -cause the girl is true to the generation X, new age of raging war of truth with raw emotion. The difference between Red Summer and her peers, a degree in *wordolgy* to back it up.

I've been waiting...with a gift to weave words and a powerful stage presence, Red Summer is acid rain poured onto a page ...fluid, with one liners and technical style packed in one drip from her pen. She kills you with a "matter-of-fact" truth in conversational tonality, like two girlfriends having a pajama party - makes you talk back at the line breaks "Girl stop playing, for real?" And anyone who's ever gone through the back and forth ups and downs of a relationship will find themselves pissed off at how she knows your life the way it seems she does.

From the opening narrative prose spoken by Katie – flight attendant of "*Git Yo Shit Right Airline*," Red Summer weaves you through a poetic novel. You hear Goapele' – her identified inspiration, in the rhythm of the falling in love with love and a person, rhyming her way through her...*Little Secrets*, coming out as a Muslim lesbian teacher, the inner workings of a day in the life of a woman who loves a particular woman, settling down in the evening happy to be a lesbian for another day. Technically sound haikus with a twist keep flow between long performance pieces with subject content (that good girls aren't allowed to talk about) like *Rain*, and needing to rinse away myself from just being a woman who worked all day. You find yourself saying, "damn, I wish I had written that."

And just when you think love can't get any better, it doesn't, Katie interjects with her special flight announcement, foreshadowing the turbulence that sometimes happen during a flight – and Red Summer takes you on the bumpy ride of a relationship in trouble, and what happens when there is betrayal. Like all good novels with a suspenseful plot, you can't put it down. You flow between poems like *The Settlement* and *Rape* all twisted in the opposite of their beginnings cause you can't really call anything a beginning if it doesn't connect to an ending.

This Just In and *Back* let you know that everything over, ain't over, until it's over. Chapter Three is filled with revelations and as my favorite professor used to say, "Claiming yo' space". Red Summer *Rambles After Heartbreak* , (but just before healing) cause she knows poets can't suffer in silence. Eventually writing through it, she will return to the self she was. Then, the *Bough Breaks*, summing it up with a line that I even had to pause to breathe for...I hate her for not knowing that she did not love me....

Chapter Four – yes Katie began to annoy me too– but hey the truth hurts and *the crack in my resolve* made me question my own reasons for trippin, cause truly knowing that you will be confused is indeed *Progress* in the back and forth of getting back together. And breaking back apart

Finally, *owning your own shit* is at the end of every lesson learned and coming to terms with the fact that relationships sometimes end in *Full Circle*, so sing *Hallelujah* not for what was, but for discovering what really is. And for knowing that even then, it's ok and so are you.

Hooray to Red Summer for giving a comprehensively close examination to the mental, emotional and physical joys and ills of relationships.
I've mentored many girl poets into women wordsmyths in the house of POW-WOW, but this one, I claim as my own.

A proud mama
C.C. Carter

Introduction

I often tell my students that it is not the fear of failure that prevents us from living our dreams… it's the fear of success. I heard that once and it resonated with me. I am a procrastinator. Proud and strong. And had it been left up to me, this book would still be sitting on sheets of notebook paper waiting for its time in the sun. Lately, however, people have been *pulling my card* and challenging me to stand on what I say I believe in. Put my money where my mouthpiece is. Say what I have hidden for so long. Put it all out there and let Universe do her thang with it.

I am at a place where I am no longer comfortable just getting by. These last two years have been ones of purging and purifying for me. I am able now to see what has endured and withstood the test as testimony. I am so blessed. I have love, music, art, friends, family and a community around the globe that has welcomed me with open arms. For that, I am so grateful.

This book is dedicated to all of the women who taught me about healing and revealing and being vulnerable again. I thank you for believing in me, loving me, trusting me and hurting me when necessary to bring about the required change.

To my muse, who has opened my eyes to so many things I had overlooked before.

To my daughter, who allows me to be myself and demands it when I falter.

To my mother, who showed me how love can endure all things.

To my "otha" momma, who scooped me up and blew wind beneath my wings.

To the women who taught me through trial and error, what love is and isn't.

To the women who have allowed me to see them love, lose and love again.

To my friends who are the reasons I still have hair, breath and some sanity left.

To the men who give me strength and faith that there are still a few who exist.

And to the men who did only what they knew to do… hey, better luck next time.

Finally, to all of you who have made me feel at home wherever I am, thank you.

I would like to introduce you all to…

Red Summer

The Journey

Katie I	6
Introducing… Red Summer	7
First Person	8
Shhh	9
punk	10
oooh girl…	12
Thank you	14
Blasphemy	16
My Little Secret	17
Phases	18
On Being a Lesbian	20
Rain	21
Breakfast	22
Spoiled the Whole Bunch	23
KatieII	24
Before	25
menstrualsituation	26
retail	27
rape	28
Turning Point	31
Katie III	32
Glass House	33
This Just In…	35
The Witness	36
Before the Lesson…	36
The Damn	37
Silence	39
Rambling after Heartbreak	41
hi, my name is…	47

Back	50
When the Bough Breaks	52
Progress	53
Katie IV	54
Untitled #1	55
The Crack in my Resolve	56
Sweet Misery	58
Indecisive	59
Suicide Note #7	60
Break Down	61
Katie V	62
Burden	63
I've Lost It	64
Sound Advice	65
To Take the Edge Off	65
Mind Reader	66
Rule Number 1	67
Plea	68
The Settlement	69
Full Circle	70
Buttafly	71
Only Love	72
Love Hurts	73
…to the swift, nor the strong	74
Hallelujah	76
Katie VI	78

Hello, and thank you for choosing *Get Yo Shit Right* Airlines.
My name is Katie and I will be your attendant for this flight.
I ask that you take a moment to review the safety regulations with me
before we take off.

In the case of an emergency,
insecurity
or extremely ignorant behavior,
exits have been clearly marked and are located at any point in this cabin.

If you are *already* seated in an exit row,
you *will be* required to alert other passengers of your plans and intentions.

You may also be responsible for assisting other passengers
who wish to exit as well.

If you **do not** feel that you can handle this responsibility,
please be honest enough to *identify* yourself
so that you may be reseated.

Passengers, who may not be able to read the clearly marked signs,
should be alerted to more *subtle* signs
using hand and body language.

However, please be advised that signs that are inferred,
intended
or suggested
are the responsibility of the ~~passive~~
I mean passenger who sends that message.

Introducing... Red Summer
(for Jackie)

I start off every day listening to Goapele'
Cause it feels like I'm getting closer to my dreams
And it seems like I can't go a day
Without poetry

If I got shot and lost all my blood
Poetry would still flow in me
If I was a slave during plantation days
Poetry would be thirteen runaways
running toward brighter days

And it's funny
Like a short girl rolling in a red Hummer
It's gonna be a Red Summer
Cause Poetry is the difference
Between the overcome
And the overcomers

First Person
(for my Muse)

she is a poet who refuses
to write in first person

prefers pronouns
like the all powerful "they"

verse after verse of "the man's" involvement
in oppression
patriarchal systems and economic depression

She is a narrator
third person limited
twice removed
from any emotional connection to the subject matter

never understanding
why the only subject that mattered to me
was her

this poet
who refuses to write in first person
ironically
was the first person to make me feel
like I exist

Shhh

my life was built on secrets

i don't wanna live that way anymore

my art is where i find my truest self

she wants me not to tell

not broadcast my experience
on reality tv

not download my life
on the web

not publish it on public pages

i say

if i am not going to tell the truth

what then
shall i tell

punk

i aint afraid to admit that i'm scared
i want you to know

cause what you're saying sounds good to me
and you look good to me
and what you're doing feels good to me
hell, you even smell good

and i know all this good has to come with some bad
it's the universal law of balance

the farther i let you take me
the longer it'll take me to get back

so, i ain't afraid to admit that i'm sacred
i want you to know

cause then you can't say that i didn't tell you
and you become responsible for every lie you tell
for every time you are careless with my heart
for everytime you say you will
and you don't

you carry some of the burden since i already told you that
i am fragile
i bruise easily
and i don't heal very fast

so, i will hold on much longer than i should
long enough for you to see my delight
turn into desperation
and for your eyes to turn from passion
to pity

and you'll fuck me because you know you can
and i'll let you because i know you will
and we both will grow tired of the monotony
of feeding our dysfunctions with each others misery
and eventually
we'll leave

and i ain't afraid to admit that i'm scared
i want you to know

because the other possibility is that you will learn to love me
that you will do it well
with skill and care
and concern for my feelings and my health and my well being

that you will love me whole
embracing my idiosyncrasies
and kissing away my insecurities
leaving me with no other option than to love you back

then i will have to admit that i don't know how to love someone
who doesn't secretly wish to see me learn my lesson
who isn't trying to show me
that i'm not all i'm hyped up to be
and that all of this is new to me

but i aint afraid to admit that i'm scared
i want you to know

oooh girl...

she said she just likes to look at me
covered me with adjectives
she said were all inadequate
and though she be emcee
it left her speechless just to look at me

"even walkin round the house in jeans
you be mean
when you do your thing
and i just like to look at you"

and i had to admit
i like watching her watch me too
she be looking hungry
like it's the day after ramadaan
and i'm a buffet
but we aint even at the appetizers yet
i'm still trying to get her to look at the menu
decide what she really wants
and all she keeps saying is "you"

i try to fight the urge to blush
cause i feel like i'm gon spontaneously combust
if she looks at me another second
she wants seconds
and dessert
and a doggie bag for a midnight snack
i'm trying to get us back
to the topic
but she won't stop it
she just keeps   looking at me

feels like she can see through me
deep into me
said "you've cast your pearls unto the swine
now it's time to cast your burdens down
and when you need peace of mind
you can have a piece of mine"

then she offered me
a heaping helping of reciprocity
whole-heartedly
it startled me
to have her give it so freely
i just knew there had to be a catch
some invisible strings attached
till she said
"i don't want your virtue
and i don't want to hurt you
so you can keep your pants zipped
and i'd rather strip you of your doubts
than your blouse
show you what respect feels like
and what love is all about"

i damn near fell out
so if it's game... count me in
i'll play for the shirts and the skins
might even let her win
just to hear that shit again

she said she just likes to look at me

Thank You

I want to thank you for making this easier for me.
I see you walking with your masculine ways
and I'm appreciative of all the fights you had to fight
in order to be able to walk so smoothly.
I love you because they call you stud,
butch, aggressive, dyke
and every knock is a boost
bringing you closer to me.

I want to thank you for making this easier for me
because you wear your sexuality on the outside.
There is no question in their minds
when they see you.
When they see me,
most of the time,
they would never suspect.
When I tell them,
there are always shocked responses
like, "but, you're so pretty."
"You could have any man you wanted."
Not understanding that all I wanted
was you.
Not understanding that your beauty is the one that intrigues me.
Not understanding that your delicate balance
between masculine and feminine,
is what keeps me coming back,
keeps me wanting more.

I want to thank you for making this easier for me.
So that when people ask me am I a lesbian…
I think of you
and all the struggles you've had to endure.
All the rude comments,
all the stares from men
who wish they could be you,
because you're with me.
I think of you
and all it took for you to just be
who you are.
And I am so proud to say
Yes.

So,
I want to thank you for making this easier for me.
Because even though I am one of those girls who could pass,
Why would I?
I love being a lesbian
because I love you.
with your sports bra, loose pants,
boxer shorts, over-sized shirt,
and comfortable shoes.
I willingly walk through this fire with you
in my stiletto heals and push up bra.
For all that you have done for yourself,
you have also done for me.
And I want to thank you for making this easier for me.

Blasphemy

How many ways can you describe the beauty of a woman
without becoming redundant?
She, who filled me with her radiance,
can only be described in such a manner.

I watched, helplessly, as I submitted to her nature.
Bold and unassuming.
Fearless and vulnerable.

I saw the exquisite essence of her smile
ridding me of cynicism and bitterness.

Her sympathy and compassion, in the face of adversity,
a testimony to me.
Her grace and steadiness a lesson
in my self-proclaimed propensity for delayed gratification.

Patience, a virtue best displayed under pressure and executed in chaos.

I, who have been commissioned to teach,
stood as humble pedagogue in her presence.

Learning to love as my first lesson.
Forgiveness the second.

Becoming more Christ-like in this supposed sin
than in years of supplication and prostration.

Washed clean in her baptismal waters,
a willing parishioner to her theology.

Lines of hip-hop verses, love ballads, chords and keys are her gospel.

Bordering on blasphemy, as I felt her move beneath me.
Calling the Father's name in vain, as I worshiped her.

Mind, body and soul,
were the only trinity of any relevance.
As I sought to enter her kingdom of God.

My Little Secret

I kicked it in the village before
but this sister got me slummin'

Some brothers had beat around the bush before
but this sister, she be drummin'

A couple of people plucked at my heart strings
but this sister, she be strummin'

Been moved to hit a note or two
but this sister keeps me hummin'

I had arrived a couple of times
but this sister keeps me comin'

So, I realized that I'm strong enough for a man
but I was made for a woman

Phases

Skeptical looks from friends and family members
who view me as too old to be "experimenting" with my sexuality.

"Nearly thirty and now she wanna date girls."

"She shoulda got that outta her system in college."

"That man finally ran her off the deep end this time."

"She must remember Uncle Willie touching her."

"She just wants attention."

Maybe.

Whatever the reason, here I am.

Carrying the torch
with my flame burning bright.

Standing in the doorway of my closet.
Not ashamed of being a woman
who loves a woman,
but well aware
that Muslim, lesbian, teachers
can't sponsor after-school activities or be left alone with students because
"those gays can't be trusted around children, you know.
They definitely shouldn't be parents
and expose their babies
to all their freakish ways."

So, I kept my pride inside
and shared it only with other women
who are comfortable with themselves
and therefore, with me.

Women who remember the history teacher, who always had to touch them, in order to answer their questions and their father's friend who always commented on how they were beginning to fill out their jeans.

Women who don't think that being a lesbian means that you are automatically a pedophile

or that you'll sleep with any woman
who crosses your path.

Women who view me
as much less of a threat
and maybe one of their
strongest allies.

I hear the words,
the opinions,
the gasps of disbelief.

I feel the stares piercing my skin.
Wounding me,
but not breaking me.

I take my scars home to my lover
and she kisses away my pain.
Loves me new again.
I rest soundly in her arms.

A phase?
Maybe.

But tonight,
I lay peacefully,
lesbian
for another day.

On Being a Lesbian
(in 17 syllables)

      I
You should be thankful
that I date women
now men can like you

      II
It seems that I had
just grown tired of stroking
men's dicks and egos

      III
Who would have known that
I could love so deeply with
no penetration

      IV
It's funny how you
can get so creative with
good motivation

      V
She had more love in
the tips of her two fingers
than all dicks combined

      VI
He propositioned
"Why don't you come back to men?"
and I laughed out loud

Rain

She said I smell like rain fallen on dark earth
As she kisses my belly
she breathes in slowly
and moves around to take me in
inhale me gently

I wrestle with my own insecurity
I beg her to let me get up
and shower
to rinse away myself
so I could come back to her
as a summer breeze
freesia and vanilla
frankincense and myrrh

But she will not let me go
Won't let me scrub my skin with black soap
and lotions
and powders
She prefers me instead

She said I smell like rain fallen on dark earth
Beautiful
natural
clean

No artificial acidic toilet water
to wash away my womanness
Pretend that vinegar is better than femininity
That rose petals are better than pussy

She said I smell like rain fallen on dark earth
Eventually
I agree
that's good enough for me

Breakfast

i rarely hug people on days like these
i don't want to walk away smelling of their cologne
or perfume

cause i tasted you this morning
and all day i have walked around
catching slight whiffs of you

tiny remnants of you
left on my lips and chin

found reasons to touch my face
so the scent of you on my fingers
could fill my nose again

no thick lotions on days like this

nothing to come between the memory of you
early in the morning
as we greet the day in our own way

Spoiled the Whole Bunch

my girl brought home a bad apple
from the cheap food store

it was green on the outside
and rotten at the core

there were no seeds inside
just a rock and a stone

it was big and juicy
but bitter to the bone

Hi, Katie again, here with a few rules for flying *Get Yo Shit Right* Airlines

Carry on baggage must be confronted, addressed
and properly dealt with.
Then, all remaining issues
and insecurities
should be stowed and locked away in the overhead compartments
provided.
Please be aware
that bags carried on this flight should be *as small* as possible
to accommodate the limited space
and prevalence of baggage carried on by *other passengers.*

Electronic devices
as well as latex,
plastic,
rubber,
glass,
leather,
liquid,
foam
and other imaginative materials
may be used during this flight.
But **please** consult with a *uniformed attendant*
and any passengers traveling with you for information on their proper use.

We ask that all passengers seat themselves comfortably
and fasten their seat belts securely.
Belts or straps should be worn low and tight
with all buckles,
knots,
snaps,
zippers,
buttons,
Velcro
and other fastening devices
placed properly as to not scratch, bruise, cut,
or otherwise harm other passengers who may have to explain these
occurrences to employers,
co-workers,
family,
friends,
or authorities of some kind.

Before

Sometimes
I wish that I had loved you
before the ones
who took pocketfulls of you home
to store in shoeboxes beneath their beds

That my kiss had made you believe
in happily ever after

That you remembered my touch
during passionate fits of poetry
and prose
and masturbation

It's hard not to feel cheated by a writer who can not
will not
cement your smile between blue lines
on white sheets

And I wish that I had been one of the ones
lucky enough
to love you

before

menstrualsituation

today is one of the rough days.

i'm trying my best not to tire of this perpetual cycle
of cycles.

periods, period.

loving women is an impossible task

every 28 days.

retail

love is a gift that comes with no receipts and no tags.
so, if you went and got it and now you don't want it,
all you can do is throw it away
or give it away.

cause if you hold onto it,
knowing you will never use it,
it will just keep your space too crowded for the new,
cute lil love you've had your eye on
in the next window.

rape
(a virtual experience)

never thought rape would come around again,
but i see all rape aint physical.

the emotional kind is way more sinister,
cause rape is about power after all,
control.

just lay there and let her fuck you.
act like you like it.
smile.
thank her for giving you the opportunity to let her fuck you.
be grateful.
sincere.
don't say shit.
don't fight back.
don't say no.
stop.
don't back her the fuck up off you.

just lay there and let my best friend fuck you.
and act like it don't hurt.
act like you like it.
act like you like her.
act like you want it.

you think she hurt you?
you'll know pain when i'm done.

cause i know all the ways to hurt you.
i've studied you,
watched you,
listened to you tell me all the ways to get to your private places.
so, i know.

and if you don't let my best friend fuck you.
i'll show you,
what pain is all about.

cause i know all i gotta do is leave you,
that's your biggest fear isn't it?

never thought rape would come around again,
not since i stopped fucking with men...

but i learned that all rape aint physical
some rape aint got shit to do with sex.

some fucking is mental,
social,
political,
emotional,
figurative.
but it is still painful,
destructive,
demoralizing,
unavoidable,
unexpected,
undeserved.

never thought rape would come around again
especially, not at the hands of the advocate.
powerful words from the "pull-pit" of righteousness,
contradicted by back door actions.

there is not enough denial
and shifting of the blame
to erase the manner in which you fucked me.
then relaxed in the soothing notion
that i got what i deserved.
that i was just asking for it.
that my own need and desire for love set me up.
not you,
or your best friend who offered me up to you.
vulnerable,
hoping that i would be handled gently by the one that i trusted and loved.

instead,
she delivered me to you on a platinum platter.
for you to fuck as you choose.
and she turned away.
so as not to have to see my face
writhing in agony.
she walked away
and blamed me for being fuckable.

it was, after all,
my fault
that her friend wanted,
desired to fuck me so badly.

so, this was no longer about her.
just me.
with her best friend shoving her entire fist inside my soul.
fucking me with all her might.
trying to destroy me.
kill me.

but since she didn't,
my love looks at me with disgust
for being fucked so ravenously
and having the nerve to survive.

my love,
turned to disgust
because i had the audacity to live,
to walk away and tell my tale.
our secret.

now, you have no idea what to do with this useless piece of trash
you have inherited from your best friend.
the blind faith and innocence replaced by the sarcasm and pessimism
you both passed on to me.

you don't want me back all used and battered,
don't wanna face the guilt of what was done.
don't wanna take any credit.
shoulder any blame.
or even admit that what happened to me was wrong.

what offends you is just my nerve
to stand up and fight for myself.
to get her fist out of my ass,
her knife out of my back.

never thought rape would come around again.
especially with all my clothes on
and over the internet.

Turning Point

She packed a bag before she left to hang out
with her ex
now friend

I realized that
not tripping
and not caring
are twins

they look just alike

and can fool you
when they want to

"Be careful"
I warned

she smiled

and left anyway

I smiled too

and went to bed

Hi, Katie again.

Emotional Seat Belt signs (ESB) have been illuminated.
So, please be aware that reassurance,
validation,
and ego stroking *may be* required.

Once we have reached our desired altitude
and trustworthiness has been established,
the ESB sign will be turned off
and you may feel free to move about the cabin.

In the event of turbulence,
ex-lovers,
evasiveness,
and other shady behaviors,
the ESB sign will be illuminated
and you will be required to return to your seat
or senses immediately
and fasten your ~~shackles~~
I mean seat belt until trust has been restored.

At our desired altitude,
you may experience increased cabin pressure.
Passengers traveling with you may ask probing and personal questions,
increase expectations,
require personal sacrifice,
desire declarations of commitment
and request various selfless acts.

Please *do not* become alarmed,
as you will become adjusted to these activities in time.

Glass House

I live in a glass house.

A beautiful glass palace that took me years to build.

I used to be like you.
In homes of brick
and mortar
and wood
and clay
and layers of insulation
and drywall
and plaster
and paint
and wallpaper.

And finally I decided that I want to be free from all that.

Not worried or afraid of the outside world.
No barriers
or blinds
or curtains to cover me.

I would like to say that I did it for some enlightened reason,
that some higher-level evolutionary experience took place
and changed my reality.

But the truth is,
I was just tired of hiding.

So when I met you,
after years of tearing down old structures and erecting this new,
glass house,
there was nowhere for me to go, that you could not see me.
I was open to you.

You were so used to the game of finding and uncovering,
that the reality of this openness frightened you.

You thought I was faking,
putting on a show.

Some kind of narcissistic exhibitionist who gets off
on letting others into this sacred space.

You didn't know that it was done to relieve me of secrets and shame

And you hated me for that.
Resented me for spoiling the thrill of the hunt.

You picked up stones
and hurled them at my glass palace.

The walls shattered, but did not crumble.
Millions of cracks covered every side
as the stones you threw got bigger
and more personal.

They were meant to destroy me
for having the audacity to be this free.

But the walls didn't fall.
Instead, the cracks you covered me with
reflected the sunlight in all directions.

Though, now, it is more difficult to see inside,
from a distance, you cannot tell that my house is made of glass.

Cause the cracks and lines left from the stones you threw,
made it look like diamonds.

This Just In…

Thanks Ken.

This just in...
Regardless of the way things used to be,
Astronomists, Biologists, and Meteorologists all agree.

The world *officially* does not revolve around yo ass.

I repeat,
the world *OFFICIALLY* does not revolve around yo ass.

More on this shocking news at 10.

Now, back to you Ken.

The Witness

I was there.
I saw the whole thing.
I tried to stop it,
But I didn't know how.
What would you do if you saw a wild animal pounce on someone?
Saw the savage desperation in their eyes,
heard the blood-thirsty screams?

I was there.
I saw the confusion on the girl's face
as she struggled to make sense of what was happening to her.
Saw her fight back
and wrestle herself free
from the death grip she was held in.

I was there.
I saw the pain she was going through
as she struggled with her decision not to strike back.
Chose to honor her humanity instead.
I saw her leave and close the door behind her,
locking the wild animal in her cage.

I was there.
I saw the whole thing.
It played over and over in my head,
as I sat alone on our bed,
among the cast off bedding,
broken decorations,
and cracked lampshade.
I tried to regulate my breathing,
massage my bruised hand,
properly word my apology
and figure out
what the hell just happened.

The Damn

I want to cry
but the tears won't come

I'm out of practice
of feeling anything but numb

I don't show my emotions
just teeth and gums

So used to being emotionally unfed
I learned to get full on crumbs

Before the Lesson Could Come

i want to write of her
but sometimes pride will not lend itself to rhyme

both love and hate have come so quickly

so forcefully into my life
my heart

i hate her for not knowing
that she did not love me

she should have known
and told me often
instead of trying
or lying

never loving i could have understood

loving and stopping is inconceivable

Silence

held captive by the silence we've created
knowing this is not the future we'd envisioned
how did we get so far
so fast

square feet
reduced to inches
as stubbornness
closes the lid
on the boxes
we've chosen to live in

poets cannot suffer in silence
drives us crazy
we go insane

so we fill
our silent days and nights
with company
and leaving
smoking
drinking
tv
and music

anything to fill the gap left
by not loving
or at least being loving

every now and then
i break the silence
pierce the thickness between us

wish her a safe journey
wish her luck on her interview
throw a blanket over her
as she shivers
indignantly
in the basement

she reminds me
that things aint the same

like i couldn't tell

i remind her that i am not a monster
no matter what she wants to believe

i will return to the self i was
before reality set in
before love turned to leaving
and softness turned to silence

we leave in silence
as we stay

for yet another day

Rambling after Heartbreak
(…and just before healing)

i'm full of words today

thoughts of leaving and staying

i'm choosing to remember the good things now

the bad are too heavy to carry

words scribbled on unlined paper
faces drawn over blue lines

laying on the couch
way back in the corner

or with cheeks pressed on bare bellies

she is gone for a while

and i see that
this is what my house will be like without her here

the ghost of her still lingers
haunts me in all the places
where we shared ourselves

i painted a butterfly on her breasts
she
an orchard on my back

we stood in the rain
as i prayed for strength
for both of us

she is all music
colors
rhyme

i
soft whispers
cool breezes

water love turned tidal wave

memories of the love i gave
the love i have to believe she tried to muster

"too strong not to be reciprocated"
she told me once

so
i'm sure it was
at least for a while

she

so much of me

i tried to hate her for not being able to see

or not wanting to
anymore

i wanted her to feel
with me
what i was feeling

wanted her to hate me too

now
in the absence of her

a dark cloud of smoke
blown away

i can see more clearly
the me
i had become

i don't like her
(me)
either

i see why she couldn't stay

see why i can't either

time now

to move on to who i am supposed to be

now that i know there is a such thing as love

that it moves
with me through life
in different forms

teaching me of myself

using others

pretending to be human
really angels
sent by the one who sends

to reveal the many sides of me

then they are gone

and i am left with myself

and the lessons

i'm choosing not to hate her now

her choice may come later
i'm sure

but that is to be expected

not enough time between loves

hadn't really let go of the last
hadn't healed yet
didn't believe again yet
wouldn't trust again yet

maybe she never will

but
i will not carry the guilt for that

only for not being able to speak
when i should have

express my pain
in a more timely manner
say no
when i meant it

and not yes
for the sake of sacrifice

she didn't need my sacrifice

i didn't either

we both needed
honesty

even when it is not easy
or pretty
or appropriate to be

we may not
have made it then either

but at least we would not have hurt so much trying

at least we would have been able to still see each other
and feel joy

i hope

but that is not the case now

what we have is the silence

and the stubborn reality of staying

when we know we both should be leaving

or if we stay

speaking
because there was so much joy here

i can see it still
even through the madness

there is peaceful sleep in our bed
even on the tear stained pillows
and that moment just before i rise

i catch a glimpse of her

and remember
how it felt to be so in love

before the silence

and the screams

and the possibility of leaving

and loving others
or at least trying
if that is possible

i did believe i was home here

i did believe in us

i won't now

though i'm ready to admit a lot of things
pride will not allow me to begin speaking

cause
i can't be sure she's ready to listen

and since i saved these words so long

it'd be a shame to waste them
on deaf ears

or blow them through one ear
and out the other side

so

in it's place

i'm choosing to remember the good things now

the bad are too heavy to carry

and my heart is too full of words
to junk it up with regret

i prefer instead

to hold on to
the excitement of giving love freely

the adrenaline rush of the possibility of love

that was good

that is what i will keep
and take with me of this

"hi, my name is…"

i talked to the counselor
she screened me
to see if i qualified
for a group

"hi red..."

she told me that
she could see
where some of my anger came from

i wondered if me seeing it too
would take it away

or if knowing
will just be knowing

i already know that the memories
of men touching me
were haunting me

that i was suffering from
the pain of losing loved ones
getting some back and losing them again

i'd never felt so alone
lonely
isolated
rejected

and angry

at all of those who said they would
but wouldn't
didn't
haven't
and won't

she was the closest
so she hurt the worst

and unfortunately
was the only one i could reach
to hurt
like she hurt me

but knowing this
does not free me

it does not take away the pain
or the silence in my house

does not bring love into my life
or peace into my heart

counselor said
she was tormenting me

that i reacted to her
because she wanted a reaction
maybe not the one she got
but one nevertheless

she said that my aggressive action
was actually passive
since i was scared i was going to go back
and i did not want her to let me come back

instead of going away
and staying away
i got her to leave
so i could not go back
when i was weak
or lonely
or needing to be touched

i told her that i was not looking for an excuse
or even a reason
i was looking for calm
resolve

i wanted to unclench my chin
and say loving words
and believe them

i want to believe
that love is not a waste of time
energy
money

hell
right now
i just want to believe that you can help me
or that someone in this group
has an answer
to the questions
raging around inside my head

Back

she's back

familiar sounds
not so familiar after so long

i kinda liked the quiet after a while

sleeping wild across the bed

the torment of my tears
and longing
without the reminder
that she is this close
and still not accessible

better that she is far away

and not close enough
to see the pain in my eyes
my face

not wanting to reach out to her
in the middle of the night
hold her
like i used to
when i could

now
i'm careful
not to cross to "her" side of the bed
not to touch her thighs
with my knees
or hold her around her waist
cup her breast
kiss the back of her neck
hold her close
while we sleep

instead
i try to keep my back to her
and try not to think of how
utterly ridiculous this whole thing is

i try not to look at her

too afraid i will see her
and she will appear to me
as she was
before
everything

went

wrong

When the Bough Breaks

what can i say today

just when i get used to silence

here comes all this noise

i don't know if it's a blessing or a curse

i wanted us to talk

but how we're talking now

we were better off being quiet

Progress

the silence is broken
with sincere words spoken

we get to the edge
but don't jump

don't trust that we will be able to
break the fall again

she says
next time
the police will come
then the ambulance
then the morgue

i want to promise there will be no next time
but i don't want to sound typical
cliché

instead i offer
ways to prevent "next times"
tell her of my change
growth
development
process

ask about hers

we slept
closer
but not yet together

morning is good
boss just gon hafta understand this one

my priorities are in place

gotta get my house in order

Hi, Katie here with another announcement from *Get Yo Shit Right* Airlines.

Lavatories are located at the front and rear of the cabin.
Therefore, you may feel free to relieve yourself of any *old shit* that may be causing you or other passengers discomfort.

If, at any time,
you begin to feel *smothered or suffocated*,
oxygen masks will descend from the ceiling.

Place the mask over your ears,
listen to the soft music and exhale.
If you are traveling with other passengers who may need assistance,
please make sure *your shit* is right
before you attempt to help someone else.

If you need assistance,
please alert a *uniformed* attendant
before consulting other clueless passengers.

In the event of an emergency landing,
In the Meantime,
Faith in the Valley,
Yesterday I Cried
and other books by Iyanla Vanzant
are located beneath your seat and may be used as a coping device.

Also, *O Magazine* is located in your seat back pocket for your convenience.
To use it,
simply remove it from the pocket,
open it,
read it,
and pull out the handy inspirational cards
to inflate your self esteem.

untitled #1

this kind of love is tumultuous

it gives
it takes

it soothes
it aches

it needs so much
but when you reach for it
it's impossible to touch

The Crack in my Resolve

i'm trippin

i know we've only been apart for a few days
and i'm already trying to find creative ways
to get myself to be able to fall asleep
without you here

so used to having you near
whenever i need someone to reach out and touch
and i didn't know i'd miss you this much

all night
i toss and turn
as my body yearns for sleep
but my mind is charged
like i got a e.nina jay cd on repeat

i tell myself consoling words
but i know they're only lies
and it seems like as soon as i close my eyes
the sun begins to rise
and i gotta drag myself outta bed
to get to work on time

now i'm facin'
the awkward situation
of trying to give these children
a quality education
while i'm suffering
from sleep deprivation

i would use my sick days
to go on a vacation
but i'd probably spend the whole time pacin'
back and forth across the floor
trying to figure out
why we're not together anymore

sittin' by the door for days
unbathed
looking like i'm on crack

scared to put down the phone
in case you call to say
you gon come back

okay
i'm exaggerating
but it seems like since we've been dating
you've been waiting
for the perfect chance to leave

and i know you get insecure
and sometimes you feel unsure

but please baby
don't take that out on me

Sweet Misery

I'm in love with the sweet misery of loving you

Obsessed with the delight of missing you

I'm grounded by the memory of you leaving

Fascinated by the pain I'm going through

What shall I do if I let go of this torture

What will I have left to drive me insane

How will I manage without this hole in my heart

And this ache at the base of my brain

I'm in love with the sweet misery of loving you

I dance in the emptiness you left behind

For how will I ever adjust to you returning my love

And what comparable agony could I find

Indecisive

i'm indecisive

like lesbians
who gave up girls
to date men
so you could be christian
then six month later
you in the gay club again

Suicide Note #7

aint nobody here to soothe my soul

gotta rub my own back
self-medicate
self-actuate
masturbate

define my own fate
while destiny
tries to get the best of me

I'm suffering from post-traumatic stress
pms
can't find a reason to get dressed
and when i do
i can't find clothes i fit into

everything sags like a heavy load
i'm about to implode
and fall in on myself

but if a human tower falls in the middle of a concrete jungle
and no one is there to hear her
will she make a sound

or will her silence drown her
once she's hit the ground

and if there's no one around
will it even matter

Break Down

parked in the driveway
i screamed to the clouds
enough already!!!!
that's enough, damn!
and smoke rolled out of my cracked car window.

the car was okay
it was my spirit that was broken
self destruction to combat
constant attacks

inhale
hold
exhale
breathe
wait for the pain to leave

Hi, Katie here.

Just wanna let you know that
meals and snacks *are offered* on this flight.

However,
if you are **not** preparing for a long flight,
please do not expect more than water and peanuts.

Federal regulations require that there be no smoking
or *any other* destructive behaviors on this flight.

Tampering with smoke detectors by lying,
sneaking,
or making dumb ass excuses
is a *punishable* Federal offense.

Burden

how often do we do the things we expect to have done?
do we treat people the way we want them to treat us?

not only put the shoe on the other foot,
but walk around in it for a while to see how it truly feels?

it's so easy,
convenient,
to think that someone else is just tripping,
crazy, insecure, immature.

harder to see that they're hurting
because of something we did.
something that we could have,
should have,
would have done differently
if we cared to see how it would affect them.
if it mattered.
if it was important
or relevant to our lives.

there is no red line on someone's forehead to show us their boiling point.
we even get mad when they're just trying to release some steam.
treat them like they don't have the right to feel
what we made them feel.

but what do you expect when you show someone the glass ceiling over
something they thought was limitless?

how would you have them react?

repression leads to revolt.
silence to slaughter.

we cannot heap a load on someone else's shoulders,
then fault them for not being able to bear the weight.

eventually,
they will break.

and what then?

I've Lost It

i used to know the purpose of all this

had all the answers
clutched tightly
in my right hand

then i set them down
to tie my shoe

and now
i can't figure out
where they ran off to

Sound Advice

they say i should choose my battles wisely
realize when it's time to put my armor away
go home
and pray

To Take the Edge Off

a message from the great and powerful oz...

you should do less meditating
and more masturbating.

that is all.

Mind Reader

she said

"there are two types of people in the world

givers
and
takers

which one you are changes
with each relationship you're in

but the roles are pretty much defined

people tend to want a relationship to be
the way it was in the beginning

so
the way it's set up initially,
is how they want it to always be..."

i wondered if she already knew
what i was going through

if our lives were on some kind of
parallel plane

or if this concept of women
dating women
just always ends up the same

Rule Number 1

the number one rule in publishing
recording
real estate
automobiles
responsibility and blame

is own your own shit

Plea

i, too

have been stuck in the middle
between bullshit and lies

the beginning being
your insecurities

you never believed how much i adore you

thought i would focus
instead
on your have nots

so
you always prepped yourself for my leaving

always assumed that i would

trying to call into existence
that which was not for you to call

i tried to get you to settle in
unpack
take your shoes from the front door
and place them under my bed

relax
and stay a while

but you never believed how much i adore you

enough to hide your flaws and still love you

enough to take them out
open them up
spread them across the table
examine them closely

and love you still

The Settlement

Right here, right now.
I'm offering you an opportunity to lay your burdens down,
cause they're looking kinda heavy sista.
and I would hate to miss the chance to help you release this stress
that seems to be eating you, beating you, heating you
and cheating you of little pieces of your spirit.
Every time you speak, I hear it.
And I aint normally the type to put my business out in the street,
but this is where you brought it, so this is where it's gon be.
It's apparent that you and i got issues.
We both have powerful spirits that we're starting to misuse.

So, I'm gon use this as a chance to discover
things about myself and others.
And I invite you to come grow with me
it's the least I can do.
And I'm gon let this be through, cause I can see you.
And no matter how dark this gets it's still see-thru
like sunglasses.
I thought it was a matter of time and after some passes,
we could get past this.
But how much of your negativity
are you going to continue to throw at me?
I offered you a ticket to ride,
but you missed the boat.
Then, tried to use me as your scapegoat.

Standing on the banks of denial,
you wanna blame your trials on me.
Never taking any responsibility
for where you ended up.
You mended up your broken heart
by picking me apart.
And I understand it,
so I let you do your thing.
But dragging my name through the mud
aint gon keep you clean.
Cause you're right in this with me.
We all played our part in it.
So we aint gon have no problem
unless you're the one starting it.

Full Circle
(for B & D)

love tugs on her
pulling her back
to where she said
she'd never go again

aint nothing common
about this
cause it makes no sense

yet she falls again
remembering
all that love promised

hoping for a return
on her investment

for something tangible
to hold onto
in the middle of the night
instead of her pillow
and her memories

she feels love tugging on her
knowing in the back of her mind
that her own hands
are the ones reaching
grabbing
pulling her back
to the love she knew
and wants again

Buttafly

she is the reason i am still here
patiently in purgatory
weeping and moaning
laughing and singing

gravity keeps us grounded
and stuck to one another
felt
but unseen

needed
but unwanted

for all that we each desired
were wings to fly
beyond gravity
beyond reason
beyond all stretch of the imagination

sometimes
our own wings
keep others from taking off

spanned wide in the air
beautiful
colorful
defying logic
and rationality

as we seek to float above reality

this time
i concede
in the hopes of watching her soar
hoping only to see the streaks of her beautiful rainbow
floating above my head
leaving music and tornados in her wake

fear not
little buttafly
and take to the skies

Only Love

Sometimes love is only love
It cannot always heal.
It cannot always change the world,
or a reality,
or a situation.

I loved you because I wanted to.
So, I can only delight in my enduring capacity to do so.
Wanting, needing and praying for a thing will not always make it manifest.
If it is not yours to have, it will never be yours.
That is my lesson in this.
I cannot change what I cannot change.

I am wiser now,
from having loved so freely.
Bitterness does not consume me.
Pity does not comfort me.
Regret does not reside in me.

I marvel at my ability to love
and accept the opportunity to do it again.
I am shaped by my love.
Fashioned into a beautiful thing by it.
My love gives me joy
and sharing it gives me peace.

I need my love
and it needs to be needed.
So, we will walk together toward whatever is waiting for us.
I hope that it is you,
but that is a path that you must choose.

Till then, my love and I must steady our steps.
More whole, more complete
and more aware that it's nature of limits and limitlessness
makes my love a gift to all who receive it.

For sometimes, love can heal all wounds,
mend all broken places
and cure all ills.
But sometimes, it's only love.

Love Hurts

love does hurt
cause it makes you feel
lets you feel
all the things you never wanted to

forces you to see the best
and worst
in yourself
and others

makes you stronger
by making you weaker

then you have to decide
what to do with the blessings
that have come from it

without the rain
there would be no life
all things would dry up
be used up
and thrive no more

storms are the quickest way
to get a lot of rain
in a little time

a lot of lesson
in an instant

they are dark
loud
violent
scary
but necessary

cause even when we think we won't
we do
make it through

and all praises are due

...to the swift, nor the strong

and… i'm off
heart rate picking up speed
as i proceed
down each corridor
don't know what i'm running for
just going

not knowing
that every turn
leads to a dead end
i turn around
and begin running again

thinking that if this time
i turn right
i just might
make it to the finish line

only to get there and find
i'm back where i began
as i concoct a new plan
it starts to feel like de ja vu

i think i've been here before

and the more i try to get away from this place
the quicker i get back to it
i find a crack in the wall
and try to bust through it
just to find
i'm back at the starting line

scrap the first route
and head out
in a new direction
do the math
chart a new path
that led right back to where i started

exhausted
broken-hearted

feeling retarded
for not being able to find
how to get out of this shit
can't decide if i should throw a fit
or just quit

wondering if i played damsel in distress
would someone come and rescue me from this mess
i've gotten myself into
trying to retrace my steps
so I don't go somewhere i've already been to
feeling like i haven't quite gon crazy
but I'm *finto*

if somebody don't come and guide me
looking like somebody dipped me in batter
and deep fried me

i'm done

but i can't tell if this race has been lost or won
all i know is

it's over

Hallelujah

Last night
I felt it break
thought it would shake my bed
clear across the room

Salt water
pain
and misery ran from the open wound

Gone get it out chile
God done troubled the water

I begged
purify me
and watched a red cloth turn white

Last night
I felt it break
been able to escape it till now

My initiation into womanhood
The elders sat back and sang
It's soooo gooooood
and it was

Felt like life
filled in all the empty spaces
Allowed love to finally seep in
all the hollow places

I didn't understand
but it felt right

Last night
I felt it break
and break
and break
and I thought
I could take no more
as the witches brew poured
from my eyes and nose and lip

I'd soar
I'd dip
I'd run
I'd trip
I flew
I stayed
I laughed
I prayed

I thought I would die right there in my bed
but I fought with all my might

Last night
I felt it break
as I pulled my soul
out of my skin

I watched myself drown in desperation
and be born again
I was baptized in the fires
to cleanse me of my sin
A ton of pressure
placed on my shoulder
created a diamond within

Nambi, Isis
Oshun, Oya
Bes, Erzuli
and Yemaya
all danced at the foot of my bed
anointed my head
and said
Rest child

When you wake
You will know what real love feels like
Last night
I realized that she does not love me

For that
I am so grateful

Hamdulillah and Hallelujah

Hi, Katie here with some sad news.

It seems that we've come to the end of our flight
with *Get Yo Shit Right* Airlines.
I hope it has been a pleasant experience for you.

Please remain in your seat
until the aircraft has come to a full and complete stop
as any *personal or emotional* injuries or regrets you sustain
will be *your* responsibility.

Be sure to remove all personal belongings
before exiting the aircraft as *anything* left behind
becomes community property
and can *only* be claimed after embarrassing visits
to *low-budget talk shows*
or after decrees from Judges Judy, Mathis or Joe Brown.

Please be cautious when opening the overhead compartment
as *old ass baggage* you **thought** was out of the way,
may have shifted to the front
during the flight.

Again,
thank you for choosing *Get Yo Shit Right* Airlines.

If *Red Summer* is where you plan to stay,
then welcome home.

If you are considering settling somewhere *else*,
I hope you enjoy your stay
before moving on to your
final destination.

Goodbye, have a nice day.
Goodbye, have a nice day,
Goodbye…

Red Summer
Both the calm and the storm

Red Summer is a Chicago native who was raised in a world of words. Coming from a talented and musical family, **Red Summer** was trained in many forms and styles of performance. She has a BA in Theater, from Grambling State University and a MA in Interdisciplinary Art, from Columbia College Chicago.

She is a model, actress, dancer, writer and performance artist. In her latest and dearest venture as a spoken word artist, she has been able to travel the globe sharing her words and thoughts.

As an educator, she has created avenues of self-expression for youth in the Chicago area. She has also worked tirelessly with LGBT youth in esteem, mentoring and educational tracking programs.

She is a poetry slam champion and has prevailed in numerous dramatic and poetic competitions. She has performed with some of today's poets of the highest regard.

Red Summer will be releasing her second collection of poetry, *Raw Sugar*, early in 2007 and has numerous projects in the near future.

Two Fingers Press is a publishing company that focuses on new work from urban writers, poets and performers. We offer artist development, promotions, performance bookings, book signings and quality printing.

Two Fingers Press is a woman-centered company that caters to artists in a personal and professional manner. We are one of very few publishing companies that feature poets, spoken-word artists and playwrights.

Our mission, at **Two Fingers Press**, is to offer publication options to writers who are:

- New
- Changing genres
- Representing under-served communities
- Too "non-traditional" for traditional publishing houses

For information on upcoming projects, performance schedules, booking information and to purchase **Two Fingers Press** products, visit us online.

www.twofingerspress.com.

www.ingramcontent.com/pod-product-compliance
Lightning Source LLC
Chambersburg PA
CBHW051703090426
42736CB00013B/2511